ACO-5763

Apt

11/07 = 5€ 4/06 (01)   10/01

MADE IN THE
U.S.A.

RECYCLED PAPER

From Start to Finish

Samuel G. Woods

Photographs by Gale Zucker

BLACKBIRCH PRESS, INC.
WOODBRIDGE, CONNECTICUT

Special Thanks

The publisher would like to thank Peter Marcalus of Marcal Paper for his generous help in putting this project together.

Published by Blackbirch Press, Inc.
260 Amity Road
Woodbridge, CT 06525

e-mail: staff@blackbirch.com
Web site: www.blackbirch.com

Printed in Singapore

10 9 8 7 6 5 4 3 2 1

Photo Credits: All photographs © Gale Zucker.

Library of Congress Cataloging-in-Publication Data
Woods, Samuel G.
Recycled paper / by Samuel G. Woods.
    p.   cm.
    Includes index.
    Summary: Demonstrates how waste paper is recycled into useful household products at the Marcal paper mill.
    ISBN 1-56711-395-8 (hardcover : alk. paper)
    1. Waste paper—Recycling—Juvenile literature. 2. Recycled products—Juvenile literature. [1. Waste paper—Recycling. 2. Recycling (Waste) 3. Recycled products.] I. Title.
TS1120.5. W66   2000
676'.142—dc21   00-008124
                                        CIP

Contents

The United States creates more garbage than any other nation in the world. Even China, which has four times as many people, creates less waste than America.

On average, Americans throw out about 210 million tons of waste every year. The heaviest portion of that waste is made up of paper and paperboard products. It is a good thing that paper is also the most recycled waste material. About 40% of all paper waste is recycled each year.

How does all that paper get recycled and re-used?

Tons of paper waste, stacked and ready for recycling.

3

Making Paper From Paper

At Marcal Paper Mills in Elmwood Park, New Jersey, more than 150,000 tons of recyclable paper is processed each year.

Magazines, school papers, flyers, and thrown-away mail make up a large portion of recyclable paper.

4

Left: *Huge bales of paper are delivered to the Marcal factory.*
Below: *The bales are opened before the paper is processed.*
Bottom: *Paper towels are just one recycled product that Marcal produces.*

Using recyclable paper, Marcal produces about 12 million cases of paper products annually. Paper towels, napkins, facial tissues, and bathroom tissue, are just a few of the many things that can be made from recyclable paper.

5

The main goal in paper recycling is to separate the usable fibers from the printed colors and coatings. The fibers are called cellulose fibers. Before this material is turned into paper, cellulose fiber is the natural cell material inside a tree. When paper is recycled, it helps to preserve natural resources by preserving trees.

Recyclable paper is first mixed with hot water and detergents in a huge mixing vat, called a pulper.

18 Tons of Mush

The first part of the recycling process is to "de-ink" the recyclable paper and turn it into a pulpy mush. Marcal is one of only a few companies that can recycle papers with all kinds of colored inks into household tissue products. To get the ink out, the paper is thrown into a large vat of hot water and detergents. This liquid is heated to about 110 degrees Fahrenheit. The hot liquid soaks the coatings off the paper and dissolves it into a gray mush, or pulp. When it is full, this vat can hold about 18 tons of pulp!

Recyclable paper is stirred into the pulper until it is completely covered.

Screen to Clean

After soaking in a mixture of water and detergent, the gray pulp is sprayed through a series of different-sized screens. This removes more elements, such as ink particles, glues, and other coatings. As the pulp is screened, it gets cleaner and brighter. From here, the pulp is pumped into another vat. There, all of the remaining non-usable elements are removed.

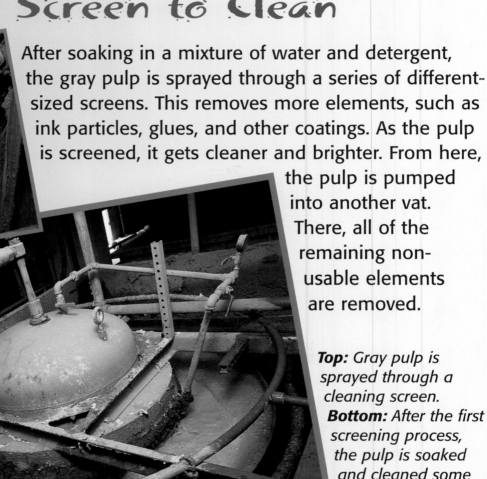

Top: Gray pulp is sprayed through a cleaning screen.
Bottom: *After the first screening process, the pulp is soaked and cleaned some more.*

From a control room, technical workers keep a close eye on the whole pulp-cleaning process. They watch to make sure that, at each cleaning stage, the pulp meets quality standards. They also make sure that the proper water temperature is maintained. That is important to completely clean and pasteurize the pulp.

In the control room, workers monitor the temperature and volume of the tanks and vats.

9

Bright White Pulp

After the cleaning process is done, all the color from the inks has been washed out. The clean cellulose fibers are now bleached to make them bright white. Every hour, the white pulp is tested for purity and quality.

Above: *A small amount of clean pulp is gathered and mixed in a small vat. The vat bottom has a fine mesh screen.*
Left: *Bright white pulp made from recycled paper.*

10

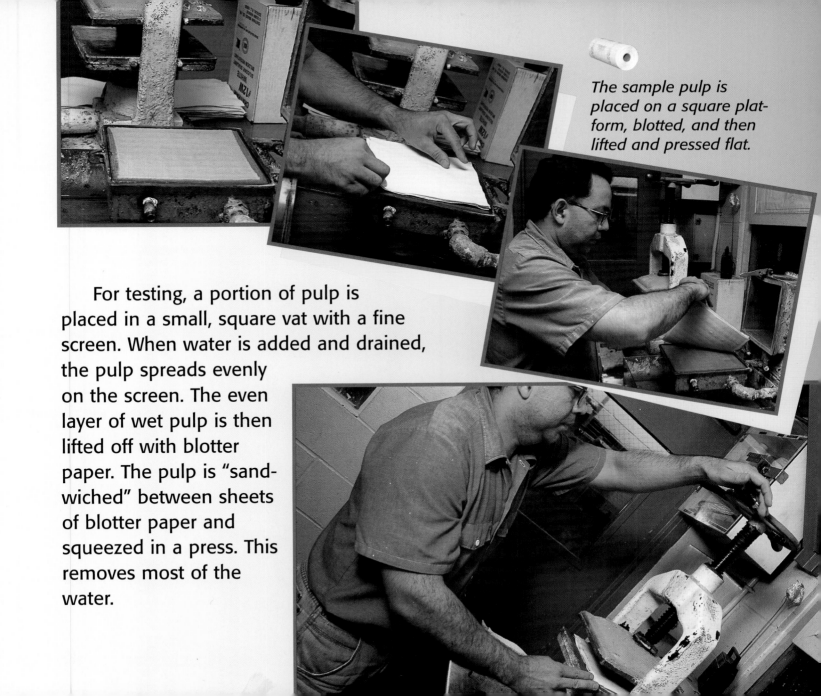

The sample pulp is placed on a square platform, blotted, and then lifted and pressed flat.

For testing, a portion of pulp is placed in a small, square vat with a fine screen. When water is added and drained, the pulp spreads evenly on the screen. The even layer of wet pulp is then lifted off with blotter paper. The pulp is "sandwiched" between sheets of blotter paper and squeezed in a press. This removes most of the water.

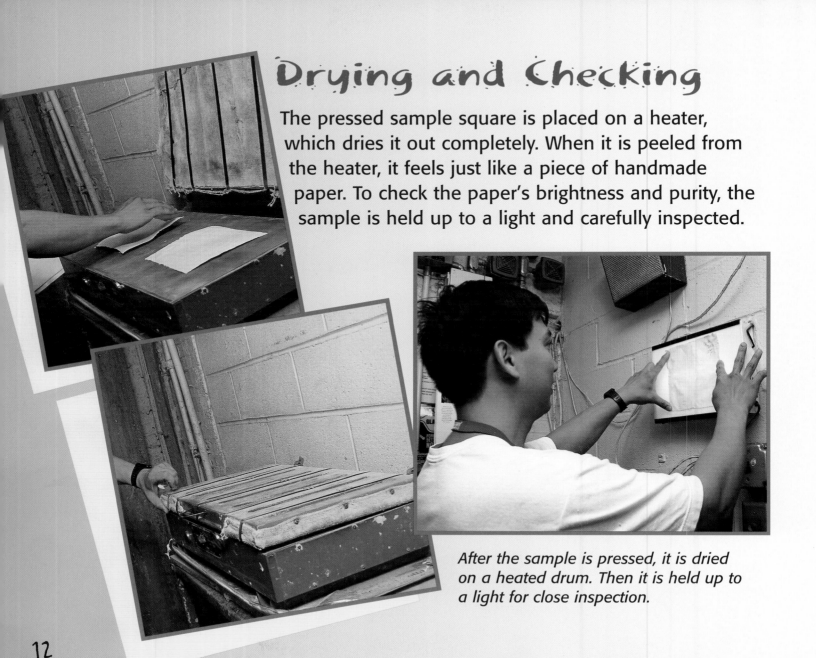

Drying and Checking

The pressed sample square is placed on a heater, which dries it out completely. When it is peeled from the heater, it feels just like a piece of handmade paper. To check the paper's brightness and purity, the sample is held up to a light and carefully inspected.

After the sample is pressed, it is dried on a heated drum. Then it is held up to a light for close inspection.

Paper Pioneer

Nicholas Marcalus, Sr.

Even though the Great Depression was crippling most American businesses—Nicholas Marcalus decided to start his own company in 1932. He had already invented what we know today as modern rolled wax paper. He was also a skilled engineer and a gifted businessman.

Soon after he opened his paper mill, Marcalus developed his own unique method for producing high-quality products from recycled paper. From that point onward, the Marcal Paper Company became known as the leader in recycled paper products.

Today, Marcal continues to develop new and unique ways to use recycled paper. Under the direction of Robert L. Marcalus and Nicholas R. Marcalus (the founder's son and grandson), the company employs more than 1,000 people. Its huge Elmwood, New Jersey, facility takes up more than 2.25 million square feet!

1939 delivery truck

Big Sheets of Paper

While the small, square sample is being tested for quality, paper is being made in the factory. There, paper is made on large, multi-million-dollar machines. Cleaned, brightened pulp is sprayed onto a huge belt-like screen. Just as was done for the small sample, water drains through the screen, and the pulp is squeezed by rollers to remove water.

Pulp is sprayed onto large screens. Then, a huge paper-making machine drains the water from the cellulose pulp fibers.

Once the liquid is pressed out, the paper passes over huge, hot metal cylinders. Heated to more than 600 degrees Fahrenheit, this is the final drying step. A long blade lifts the fast-moving sheet of paper off the dryer. More than a mile of new paper is made this way every minute.

Heated rollers press and dry the large paper sheets.

15

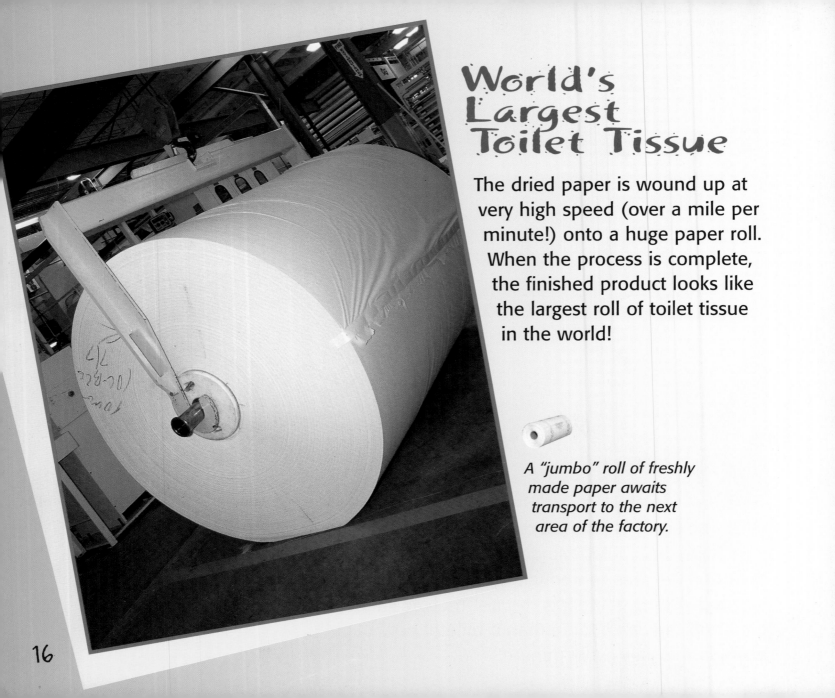

World's Largest Toilet Tissue

The dried paper is wound up at very high speed (over a mile per minute!) onto a huge paper roll. When the process is complete, the finished product looks like the largest roll of toilet tissue in the world!

A "jumbo" roll of freshly made paper awaits transport to the next area of the factory.

16

A full "jumbo" roll of paper weighs between 2 and 3 tons. It requires a large clamp truck to move it.

17

More Testing

Before the paper is printed and packaged, a sample of the finished paper is tested once again. This time, it is tested for different, important qualities. One machine holds the layers of paper and pulls them tight to test strength. Other tests check the thickness, brightness, and weight of each tissue sample that comes from the "jumbo" rolls.

A special machine tests the strength of a finished paper sample.

A worker puts a paper sample to the test, checking weight, thickness, and brightness.

19

Re-Recycling

Most paper recycling processes create some waste, but not at Marcal! All the printed coatings that are removed when the pulp is cleaned are collected in a large vat. These coatings are made mostly of clay. Marcal recycles this clay and makes a whole new line of absorbent products out of it!

Gray, mineral-like clay solids are a co-product of papermaking.

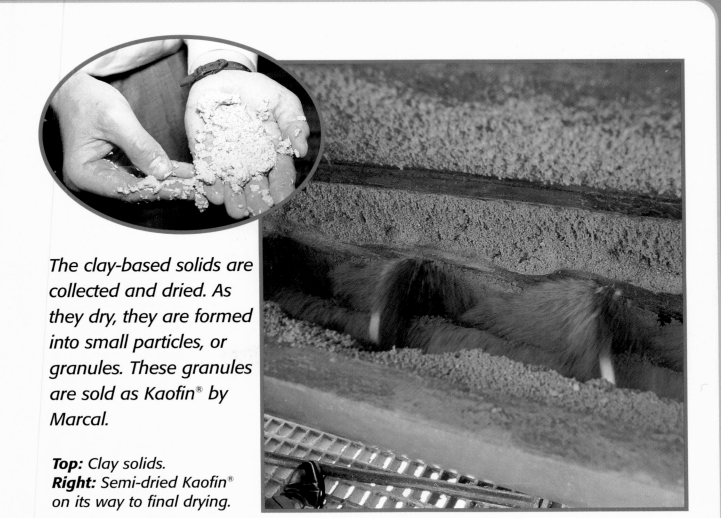

The clay-based solids are collected and dried. As they dry, they are formed into small particles, or granules. These granules are sold as Kaofin® by Marcal.

Top: Clay solids.
Right: Semi-dried Kaofin® on its way to final drying.

To package finished Kaofin®, the dried granules are sorted by size. Then the granules are bagged.

Kaofin® products are sold to a wide variety of industries for many uses. Kaofin® is used as an all-purpose absorbent, to soak up chemical or oil spills. It is also sold for use in making cat litter.

This granulated product is being tested to make sure it meets quality standards before it is sold as an all-purpose absorbent.

Kaofin® is also sold to large farms. There, it is used as a high-performance animal bedding product that absorbs animal wastes in large dairy barns and horse stalls. Farmers can also dispose of the used Kaofin® easily—it can be used to make compost, and it is completely biodegradable.

Left: Kaofin® *is bagged before shipment.*
Bottom: Bulk Kaofin® *for farm use is loaded into a large truck.*

23

Printing and Patterning

Near the end of the papermaking process, huge, nearly finished paper rolls are taken to an area for final processing. Here, the paper unwinds as it is fed into a special machine. Rollers guide the paper across cylinders that print a pattern on the fast-moving sheet. A second set of giant rollers presses a texture into the paper as it moves through.

As the paper is printed and pressed, a nearby machine makes cardboard tubes. Here, a long strip of cardboard is fed into a spinning device that rolls it tightly, glues it, and cuts it to a uniform length. These tubes await the nearly finished paper.

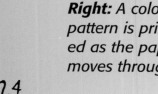

Above: Paper unrolls onto a printing machine.
Right: A colorful pattern is printed as the paper moves through.

24

Above and left: Long strips of cardboard paper are moved over a glue wheel, rolled tightly together, and are cut into finished lengths.

25

Mega-Rolls

Super-long rolls of paper towels (known as "logs") are stacked in a rack before they are fed onto a conveyor (moving) belt. On the belt, they travel through a cutting machine. This machine slices the long rolls into shorter rolls of a finished length.

Long rolls await the cutting machine.

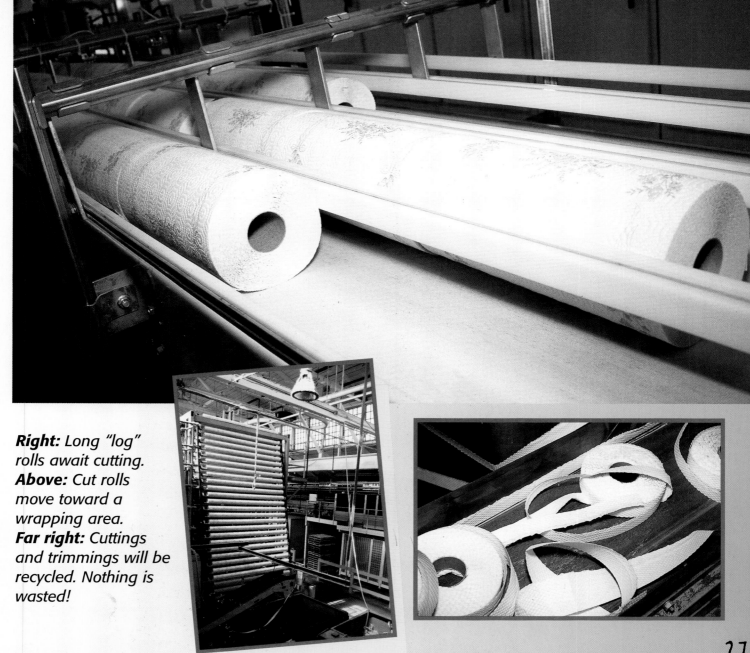

Right: Long "log" rolls await cutting. **Above:** Cut rolls move toward a wrapping area. **Far right:** Cuttings and trimmings will be recycled. Nothing is wasted!

27

Roller Coaster Ride

Once the rolls are cut, they travel through a long conveyor system that looks like a mini roller coaster.

Finished rolls head for the "roller coaster" that transports them to a packaging area.

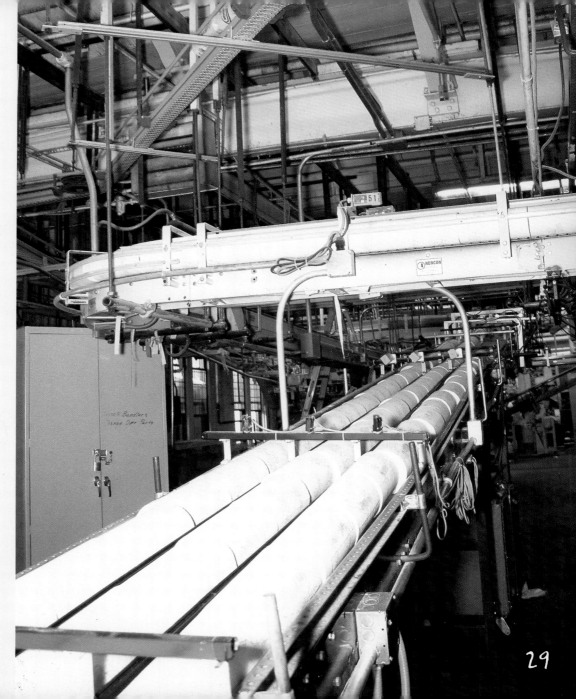

As the rolls ride along, workers inspect them. They pull rolls off the line that do not meet quality standards. The rolls that make it to the end of the roller coaster are fed into a machine that wraps them with their final packaging.

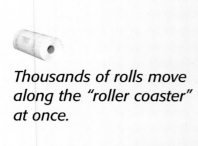

Thousands of rolls move along the "roller coaster" at once.

Brand-New Product!

Once wrapped, the rolls are collected into bundles and are placed in large shipping cartons. In these cartons, they are shipped to stores throughout the country. Eventually, they find their way into a home like yours. The recycling process is finally complete when you reach for a paper towel to mop up a spill or wipe off a countertop!

Final bundling takes place before groupings of rolls are placed in large cartons for shipping.

Glossary

Absorbent something that soaks up liquid.

Biodegradable something that can be broken down naturally by bacteria.

Blot to dry or soak up liquid.

Preserve to protect something so it stays the way it is.

Purity cleanliness; free of any marks, dust, or imperfections.

Quality grade or degree of excellence.

Texture the look and feel of something, especially its roughness and smoothness.

Vat a large tank or container used for storing liquids.

For More Information

Books

Blashfield, Jean F. *Recycling* (SOS Earth Alert). Danbury, CT: Children's Press, 1991.
Parker, Steve. *Waste, Recycling and Re-Use* (Protecting Our Planet). Chatham, NJ: Raintree/Steck Vaughn, 1998.
Stefoff, Rebecca. *Recycling* (Earth At Risk). New York, NY: Chelsea House, 1991.

Web Sites

Marcal Paper Company

This kids' site has crossword and word search puzzles, school projects, and a recycling game—**www.marcalpaper.com/marcal_kids.html**

Planet Pals

This page provides links to many schools, groups, and organizations with Earth-friendly ideas and projects—**www.planetpals.com/thinkgreen.html**

Index